LET'S FIND OUT! ENGINEERING

SOLVING REAL-WORLD PROBLEMS WITH AGRICULTURAL ENGINEERING

MARCIA AMIDON LUSTED

Britannica®
Educational Publishing

IN ASSOCIATION WITH

ROSEN
EDUCATIONAL SERVICES

Published in 2016 by Britannica Educational Publishing (a trademark of Encyclopædia Britannica, Inc.) in association with The Rosen Publishing Group, Inc.
29 East 21st Street, New York, NY 10010

Distributed exclusively by Rosen Publishing.

To see additional Britannica Educational Publishing titles, go to rosenpublishing.com.

First Edition

Britannica Educational Publishing
J.E. Luebering: Director, Core Reference Group
Mary Rose McCudden: Editor, Britannica Student Encyclopedia

Rosen Publishing
Heather Moore Niver: Editor
Nelson Sá: Art Director
Nicole Russo: Designer
Cindy Reiman: Photography Manager
Heather Moore Niver: Photo Researcher

Library of Congress Cataloging-in-Publication Data

Lusted, Marcia Amidon
 Solving real-world problems with agricultural engineering / Marcia Amidon Lusted. — First edition.
   pages cm. — (Let's find out! Engineering)
 Audience: Grade level 1–4.
 Includes bibliographical references and index.
 ISBN 978-1-68048-261-4 (library bound) — ISBN 978-1-5081-0069-0 (pbk.) — ISBN 978-1-68048-319-2 (6-pack)

1. Agricultural engineering—Juvenile literature. I. Title.

S675.25.L87 2016
630—dc23

2015034560

Manufactured in the United States of America

CONTENTS

What Does an Agricultural Engineer Do?

Engineers solve problems using science and math. They figure out the best way to create new things. Some engineers improve products. Others design things that can solve different kinds of problems. There are many kinds of engineers.

"Agriculture" is another word for farming. It includes both growing and harvesting crops and

An agricultural engineer tests the water and salt levels of the soil in an orchard.

raising animals. Agriculture provides the food that humans need to survive. Agricultural engineers do many different kinds of jobs. They improve the way crops are grown. They find better ways to raise animals. They invent new biofuels.

Some agricultural engineers work in factories. Others work in laboratories or offices. Some work outdoors in fields or forests.

Agricultural engineers help design new machines to harvest crops.

Biofuels are fuels made from plant or animal materials. One kind of biofuel is ethanol. It is made from grains like corn.

BUILDING BETTER MACHINES

One way that agricultural engineers help farmers is by building machines to help them plant, gather, and process their crops. In 1793, Eli Whitney invented the cotton gin. It helped clean cotton after it was picked. Tractors and combines make planting and harvesting easier and faster. Farmers who

A **combine** is a farm machine that collects crops in the field.

This machine picks cotton much faster than people can.

An agricultural engineer checks plants in a greenhouse to see if they are healthy.

live in dry areas also use irrigation, or artificial watering. These tools were created by agricultural engineers.

Agricultural engineers are always creating better machines for farming. Air seeders plant seeds without plowing the soil. New tractors use computers to communicate. Engineers design greenhouses that can grow more plants in the winter. Agricultural engineers help farmers produce more food faster and more easily.

COMPARE AND CONTRAST

Farmers once plowed up dirt before they planted seeds. Now they try to plant without plowing. Why would one way of planting be better than the other?

SOWING AND GROWING

Developing new types of plants means checking them regularly for growth or disease.

Agricultural engineers develop better plants. They create hybrid seeds that produce more or grow better in places where it is too dry or too wet or where the soil is poor. Hybrid seeds combine the features of different kinds of the same plant to create a stronger plant.

Genes are tiny units that carry information about an organism. They make up the material called DNA, which is found in the cells of every living thing.

A farmer and an agricultural engineer inspect a field of sunflowers.

Engineers also use genetic engineering to create better crops. In genetic engineering, the genes of a living thing are modified, or changed. Genetic engineering helps to produce crops that are stronger or more nutritious than regular crops. Some crops are engineered to prevent pests. Others have added vitamins or minerals. But some people fear that eating genetically modified food could harm people's health.

THINK ABOUT IT

Why might people be afraid to eat food that has been genetically modified?

Animals All Around

Many farmers raise animals such as pigs, cows, and chickens. Agricultural engineers can help design better ways to raise these animals. They build pens, cages, and equipment to house animals. Engineers can design better ways to handle animal waste and to keep farms cleaner. They make it easier for farmers to care for animals and keep them healthy.

Engineers also find new ways to process animals for food. Some engineers work on ways for animals to be slaughtered **humanely**. Temple Grandin is a US

It is important to keep farm animals like chickens healthy and well cared for.

Temple Grandin works for more humane treatment of farm animals.

To act **humanely** means to show caring and kindness in how others are treated.

professor of animal science. She started a company to design humane livestock handling systems. The systems prevent animals from feeling fear or pain as they are handled and led to slaughter.

COMPARE AND CONTRAST

Why would it be better for an animal to be raised in a humane environment instead of a dirty, crowded one?

WHAT'S IN THE WATER?

Aquaculture farmers raise animals and plants in water. Aquaculture can include growing and processing seaweed for food and even creating pearls. Aquaculture can take place in freshwater or salt water. Farmers also grow plants in water or some other type of liquid. This is called hydroponics. It is usually done in a greenhouse.

Agricultural engineers can improve aquaculture and hydroponics by creating new

Many crops grow well in hydroponic systems.

This salmon farm was designed to raise healthy fish to sell.

ways to move water. They design ways to keep fish and seafood healthy and help them grow faster. Engineers design earth ponds and pools for fish to hatch eggs. They may even find new kinds of crops to grow in water, such as algae.

Algae are living things that are commonly found in water. They make much of Earth's oxygen, which all animals need to breathe.

THINK ABOUT IT

Why is it a good idea to grow crops in water rather than just in soil?

LOOKING AT THE LAND

Agricultural engineers design ways to make land work better for farming. Some land is too wet, hilly, or dry for farming. Engineers can make changes in how and where crops are planted. For example, they may use contour farming to control the flow of water in hilly areas.

Studying the land and the plants growing there helps engineers find out how to improve it.

Contour farming means plowing and planting curved rows of crops on sloped lands to keep water from running straight down the hillside.

COMPARE AND CONTRAST

Why would curved rows of plants work better on a hillside? Why are they more difficult to farm than straight rows?

Agricultural engineers can address the shortage of farmland by reclaiming land that has been used for other purposes. Land that has been a swamp or lake can be dried out by constructing dams. Poor soil can be improved with fertilizers. Places that were once built on can be reclaimed by cleaning up debris.

Growing plants in curved rows can help them catch more rainwater.

FROM FARM TO TABLE

Farmers grow food, but that food has to get to the people who need it. First, the crops are picked. Then they are sent to the market. Some fruits and vegetables are taken to factories where they are frozen or processed into canned

When foods are **processed,** they are prepared or changed in a special way.

After farmers pick crops like raspberries, the berries are sent to a market or factory.

goods. Agricultural engineers find ways to make this process work better, such as storing crops and sending them to markets while they are fresh.

THINK ABOUT IT

Why is fresh food better for you than processed food?

Engineers also design better machines for preparing food. They make sure that food is safe and tasty. Engineers also want better ways to process food quickly and easily. Machines must work well so that the supply of food is always reliable. This is important because the number of people who need that food is growing.

Some crops, like raspberries, are frozen and then sent to stores.

Powering Up

It takes power to make a farm work. Tractors need gasoline or diesel fuel. Machines need electricity. In some places, electrical power is not dependable. Agricultural engineers may work to build more dependable systems for electricity in remote areas or parts of the world that do not have modern power sources.

Engineers also look for different sources of power. Energy from solar and wind power can run machines.

Solar power is the heat and light energy produced by the sun.

Wind turbines like these can create electricity for farms.

Solar panels provide energy for buildings and machinery.

Geothermal energy is heat that comes from inside Earth. In some places, it is used as an energy source. Plant materials and animal waste can be made into biomass fuel. Algae produce oil, which can also be made into biofuels that replace gasoline and diesel fuel.

THINK ABOUT IT

What sources of energy do you think are the easiest and least expensive to use?

FARMING TECH

Organizing and operating a farm involves making many decisions. Farmers today use computers to help make these decisions. Computers make it easier for farmers to gather and organize information. They can keep track of their animals. They can get weather and market information. Computers also help farmers buy and sell products and equipment and manage their money. They can also communicate with other farmers and experts.

Modern tractors have computers and GPS that help farmers with planting crops.

The Global Positioning System **(GPS)** uses artificial satellites that orbit Earth to show information about an exact location.

Computers attached to farm machinery help farmers waste less fertilizer and water.

Engineers help make all this possible.

Engineers use computer modeling to design farms that use land in the best way. They also use **GPS** to map farmland and find boundaries. It helps them create contouring. GPS technology used on a tractor helps to create straight rows and plant seeds evenly.

THINK ABOUT IT

Is it a good idea for farmers to rely on technology more than their own experience?

TENDING TO THE TREES

Forestry is the study of forests and how to manage them. Foresters plant, raise, and harvest trees. Agricultural engineers work with foresters to find better ways to manage their trees and produce wood products. They design plans for the best ways of planting trees and keeping them healthy. They study pests and how to protect trees from them. They manage trees in places like national forests. They may even start controlled forest fires to clear away brush and prevent larger fires.

Controlled forest fires can actually help new trees grow.

> **Grafting** is a process where a portion of one plant is inserted into the stem, root, or branch of another plant so that they are joined and grow together.

Agricultural engineers also create new kinds of trees or improve existing ones. They can make fruit trees bear more fruit or prevent disease. Processes like grafting create hybrid trees that combine the best parts of several species. These trees may be stronger or grow a new kind of fruit or nut.

Grafting can be used to repair injured trees or to strengthen plants' resistance to disease.

WATER, WATER EVERYWHERE

Farms and crops need a lot of water. In fact, agriculture accounts for more than two-thirds of the world's water use. Engineers must design systems that effectively use and manage water. They build waterways for irrigation without draining rivers or other water sources. They find water sources in places where there is not enough rain. They construct

Irrigation is what farmers do when they add water to their fields. The water makes their crops grow. Irrigation takes the place of rainfall in dry regions.

Irrigation systems bring water to crops growing in dry areas.

pumps to bring water up from the ground. Engineers are even building machines that transform salty ocean water into freshwater. Salt is not good for crops, but if it can be removed from the ocean water, that water can be used for irrigation.

Engineers also work to protect natural water sources from fertilizers and animal waste. These things can pollute the water sources if rain washes them off of farmland and carries them into ponds or rivers.

Desalination plants like this remove salt from seawater so the water can be used to grow crops.

FUTURE FOOD

There are more people every year. How will all these people get enough food to eat? Agricultural engineers look for ways to grow more food in less space. They also design ways to grow food in places that are now too wet or too dry for regular farming. This might mean creating crops that produce more food or can grow well in changing conditions as the world's climate keeps changing.

> The weather found in a certain place over a long period of time is known as the **climate**.

Engineers have designed farms that

New types of rice plants can grow more rice for hungry people.

work in cities, too. In some cities, small farms are planted on the roofs of buildings. These green spaces not only produce food, but they also help clean the air. In the future, some people hope to build food skyscrapers in the middle of cities.

COMPARE AND CONTRAST

Are green roofs easier than food towers for growing food in a city?

Engineering in Action

Sometimes, agricultural engineers solve problems by designing ways to help natural processes. For example, plants cannot produce crops unless they are pollinated. Usually, insects do the pollinating. But sometimes they need help. An agricultural engineer can help by transferring pollen from one plant to another by hand.

You can pretend you are an engineer helping to pollinate plants. Spread a tablespoon of baking soda on a plate. Cut out four squares of black

Bees are nature's pollinators, but sometimes they need help from engineers.

construction paper, about 3 inches (8 centimeters) square. Now try using each of the following items to pick up the baking soda: a marble, a piece of tape, a cotton ball, and a pipe cleaner. Press each item against a square of paper and see how much baking soda is transferred.

Agricultural engineers often pollinate plants by hand.

GLOSSARY

boundary Something that points out or shows a limit or end; a dividing line.

fuel A material used to produce heat or power by burning.

genetic engineering Changing the genes of a plant or animal in order to change one or more of its characteristics.

geothermal Of, relating to, or using the heat of Earth's interior, or produced by such heat.

implements Tools or machines used to perform a job.

laboratory A place equipped for conducting scientific experiments and tests.

livestock Animals kept or raised, especially farm animals kept for use and profit.

pollute To contaminate or dirty the environment with harmful substances.

population The whole number of people living in a country or region.

pump A device that raises, transfers, or delivers a liquid, especially by suction or pressure or both.

reclaim To change to a desirable condition or state.

reliable Able to be trusted; dependable.

resist To withstand the force or effect of.

seeder A machine for planting or sowing seeds.

slaughter The act of killing, especially the butchering of livestock for market.

FOR MORE INFORMATION

Books

Borth, Teddy. *Machines on the Farm*. Minneapolis, MN: ABDO Publishing, 2014.

Dickmann, Nancy. *Food from Farms*. Portsmouth, NH: Heinemann, 2010.

McNamara, Margaret. *The Apple Orchard Riddle*. New York, NY: Schwartz & Wade, 2013.

Miller, Reagan. *Engineering in Our Everyday Lives*. New York, NY: Crabtree Publishing, 2014.

Miller, Reagan. *Engineers Solve Problems*. New York, NY: Crabtree Publishing, 2014.

Montgomery, Sy, and Temple Grandin. *Temple Grandin: How the Girl Who Loved Cows Embraced Autism and Changed the World*. New York, NY: Houghton Mifflin Harcourt, 2014.

Websites

Because of the changing nature of Internet links, Rosen Publishing has developed an online list of websites related to the subject of this book. This site is updated regularly. Please use this link to access the list:

http://www.rosenlinks.com/LFO/Agri

Index